SCHOLASTIC discover more™

# penguins

By Penelope Arlon
and Tory Gordon-Harris

# How to discover more

*Penguins* is a very simple book to use and enjoy. By knowing a little bit about the way it works, you will have fun reading and discover more.

## The pages

Every page is a little bit different, but all of them will give you lots of information, stunning pictures, and great facts.

*The introduction tells you what the pages are about.*

*Labels tell you what you are looking at.*

*This symbol means that the penguin on the page is endangered and at risk of becoming extinct.*

**UNDER THREAT**

## King penguins

King penguins are easy to recognize because of the bright yellow and orange plumage on their heads and necks.

......Fully grown adult

Moulting chick.

Fluffy brown chick:

**Moulting chicks**
King penguin chicks moult, or lose their baby feathers, when they are about 10 months old.

King penguins care for their chicks for about

# Digital companion book

Download your free all-new digital book,

## Amazing Antarctica

**Log on to www.scholastic.com/discovermore**

**Enter your unique code:
RCCWNR6XCC33**

**Discover this icy continent**

*Captions tell you more about the subject.*

*Small text gives you interesting facts about the pictures.*

*Look up a favourite subject in the contents.*

**Beach sharing**
King penguins often share their beaches with enormous elephant seals. Luckily the seals don't eat them on land, so they are safe.

*Elephant seals swim fast enough to catch penguins in the water, but they are slow on land.*

····· **Elephant seal**

**KING**
*Aptenodytes patagonicus*
**HEIGHT**
97 cm (38 in)
**BREEDING AREA**
Islands around Antarctica

**Antarctica**

☐ Island populations
☐ Mainland populations

**POPULATION**
2.2 million pairs
**FEATURES**
Yellow and orange head feathers

**Find out more** ◄◄
about chicks on page 52.

**Left in charge**
King penguin chicks stay on their parents' feet for up to eight weeks. They then join a crèche. One adult keeps an eye on all the chicks in the crèche!

months – longer than any other bird in the world!

*The bottom line gives bite-sized facts and asks you questions.*

…agonicus

**HEIGHT**
97 cm (38 in)

**BREEDING AREA**
Islands around Antarctica

*The data boxes give vital information and statistics about every penguin.*

►► **Find out more**
*This takes you to another page with related information.*

**Glossary**

*Look up or learn new words in the glossary.*

**Index**

*Look up a word in the index and find which page it's on.*

**Ice floe**

**Floating islands**
An ice floe is a large, flat sheet of floating ice. Floes are found in many sizes and shapes. The surface of the ocean begins to freeze in late March, when an enormous area of pack ice forms in the bays and coastal waters around Antarctica. Most of this pack ice breaks up and melts with warmer weather, when the ice floes break off and drift away.

Ice floes are often used by penguins, especially Adélie penguins, to get between areas of ice and land. Sometimes they hitch a lift on floating ice floes, and sometimes they walk or jump across them.

**Click the pop-ups to find out even more**

**Sea life**

The sparseness of life on land contrasts greatly with the variety of life in the Southern Ocean. About 27 types of seabirds breed in the Antarctic region – including the penguins. Six types of seals frequent the Southern Ocean. Of these, Weddell, Ross, crabeater, and leopard seals breed in or near Antarctica. Blue, fin, sei, humpback, and sperm whales are also common visitors.

Fish and shellfish include cod, molluscs, and sea spiders, and researchers have found jellyfish with tentacles 3.6 metres (12 feet) long and starfish 0.6 metres (2 feet) wide.

But it is the tiny sea creatures called krill that are especially important to Antarctica's marine (sea) ecosystem – the community of living organisms and their environment. They are food for so many birds and sea animals, large and small.

Tiny shrimp-like sea creatures called krill are food for whales, seals, birds, and fishes. In turn, krill feed on plants and smaller animals.

**Encyclopedia entries packed with facts**

**Quick quiz**

**1 What is it like in Antarctica?**
Ⓐ Antarctica is sunny and warm
Ⓑ Cold, windy, and frozen
Ⓒ Warm, windy, and wet

**2 Which creatures inhabit Antarctica?**
Ⓐ Polar bears and penguins
Ⓑ Husky dogs, bears, and furry animals
Ⓒ Hardly anything - except seabirds

**3 Who lives near the volcanoes?**

**4 Why doesn't the sun melt all the snow in Antarctica?**
Ⓐ Because it snows every day
Ⓑ Sunlight is reflected back to space
Ⓒ The sun is too far away

**Fun Antarctica quizzes**

# Contents

**Consultant:** Cherry Alexander
**Art Director:** Bryn Walls
**Designer:** Ali Scrivens
**Managing Editor:** Miranda Smith
**Editor:** Slaney Begley
**Cover Designer:** Natalie Godwin
**DTP:** Sunita Gahir, John Goldsmid
**Picture Research:** Dwayne Howard, Alan Gottlieb
**Executive Director of Photography, Scholastic:** Steve Diamond

Library of Congress Cataloging-in-Publication Data Available

Distributed in the UK by
Scholastic UK Ltd
Westfield Road
Southam, Warwickshire
England CV47 0RA

ISBN 978 1407 13152 8

10 9 8 7 6 5 4 3 2 1    12 13 14 15 16

Printed in Singapore   46
First edition, March 2012 HB

Scholastic is constantly working to lessen the environmental impact of our manufacturing processes. To view our industry-leading paper procurement policy, visit www.scholastic.com/paperpolicy.

# What is a penguin?

A penguin is a bird. But unlike most other birds, penguins cannot fly. Instead they live mostly in the water. Penguins are excellent swimmers.

Emperor penguin

Penguins have feathers, just like all birds. Penguin feathers are waterproof.

Penguins' wings are like dolphin flippers, which are very good for swimming.

Penguin chicks are hatched on land and are very fluffy.

**Penguins may have got their name from the Latin word**

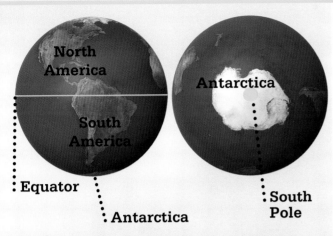

North America

South America

Antarctica

Equator

Antarctica

South Pole

## Where do penguins live?

There are no penguins north of the Equator – the imaginary line around the centre of the Earth. Penguins live in the southern half of the world, most near or on Antarctica.

## Penguin flocks

Penguins spend most of their lives in water, but they return to land to have their chicks. They often flock together in enormous groups to lay their eggs.

▶▶▶ **Find out more** about penguin colonies on page 46.

## Introducing penguins

There are 17 different types of penguins. By the end of this book you should be able to name every single one!

centimetres

85
80
75
70
65
60
55
50
45
40
35
30
25
20
15
10
5

*The fairy penguin is the smallest penguin and has slightly blue feathers.*

*The Galápagos penguin has a longer, thinner bill than most other penguins.*

### fairy penguin

LATIN NAME:
*Eudyptula minor*
HEIGHT:
46 cm
(18 in)
POPULATION:
500,000 pairs
DIET:
Small fish, squid, and crustaceans
NESTS:
Burrows or gaps in rocks lined with plants

### Galápagos penguin

LATIN NAME:
*Spheniscus mendiculus*
HEIGHT:
51 cm
(20 in)
POPULATION:
1,000 pairs
DIET:
Mullet, sardines, and squid
NESTS:
Simple burrows

*pinguis*, meaning "plump".

# More penguins

The smallest penguin is only about knee-high, and the biggest is as tall as a seven-year-old child!

*The African penguin has black feet and pink areas around its eyes.*

*The Fiordland penguin's crest runs from its bill to the top of its head.*

*The Snares penguin has a thick bill with white skin at the base if its beak.*

85 centimetres
80
75
70
65
60
55
50
45

*The rockhopper penguin has spiky feathers on its head.*

25
20
15
10
5

## rockhopper penguin

LATIN NAME:
*Eudyptes chrysocome*
HEIGHT:
58 cm
(23 in)
POPULATION:
1.2 million pairs
DIET:
Fish, krill, and squid
NESTS:
Burrows in rocky gaps

## Fiordland penguin

LATIN NAME:
*Eudyptes pachyrhynchus*
HEIGHT:
61 cm
(24 in)
POPULATION:
3,000 pairs
DIET:
Fish, krill, and squid
NESTS:
In caves or in thick, hanging plants

## Snares penguin

LATIN NAME:
*Eudyptes robustus*
HEIGHT:
66 cm
(26 in)
POPULATION:
29,000 pairs
DIET:
Fish, krill, and squid
NESTS:
Shallow nests lined with twigs and branches

## African penguin

LATIN NAME:
*Spheniscus demersus*
HEIGHT:
69 cm
(27 in)
POPULATION:
26,000 pairs
DIET:
Fish and krill
NESTS:
Burrows under rocks or low plants

**Learn to spot the types of penguins and you will really**

_The erect-crested penguin has a crest that stands up very straight._

_The chinstrap penguin is easy to spot because it looks as if it is wearing a helmet with a strap below the chin._

_The Humboldt penguin has brown feathers and a band across its chest._

_The Magellanic penguin has two black horseshoe-shaped bands over its tummy._

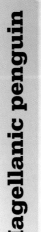

## erect-crested penguin

LATIN NAME:
_Eudyptes sclateri_
HEIGHT:
71 cm
(28 in)
POPULATION:
83,000 pairs
DIET:
Squid and krill
NESTS:
Open nests on rocky surfaces

## chinstrap penguin

LATIN NAME:
_Pygoscelis antarcticus_
HEIGHT:
71 cm
(28 in)
POPULATION:
6 million pairs
DIET:
Fish, krill, and shrimps
NESTS:
Circular nests made from pebbles

## Humboldt penguin

LATIN NAME:
_Spheniscus humboldti_
HEIGHT:
74 cm
(29 in)
POPULATION:
6,000 pairs
DIET:
Anchovies, herring, and crustaceans
NESTS:
In caves and along cliffs

## Magellanic penguin

LATIN NAME:
_Spheniscus magellanicus_
HEIGHT:
74 cm
(29 in)
POPULATION:
1.3 million pairs
DIET:
Fish, krill, and squid
NESTS:
Burrows under rocks or bushes

**impress your friends! They are all unique.**

# Even more penguins

The Adélie penguin has a bright white chest, and white circles around the eyes.

The royal penguin is the only penguin that has an almost completely white face and chin.

The macaroni penguin has orangy-yellow tassels that meet between the eyes.

The yellow-eyed penguin has a yellow stripe running around its head.

130 centimetres
125
120
115
110
105
100
95
90
85
80
75
70
65
60
55
50
45

25
20
15
10
5

**Adélie penguin**

LATIN NAME:
*Pygoscelis adeliae*
HEIGHT:
76 cm
(30 in)
POPULATION:
2.5 million pairs
DIET:
Fish and krill
NESTS:
Circles of small stones and pebbles

**royal penguin**

LATIN NAME:
*Eudyptes schlegeli*
HEIGHT:
76 cm
(30 in)
POPULATION:
850,000 pairs
DIET:
Fish and squid
NESTS:
Shallow nests scraped into sandy or pebbly ground

**macaroni penguin**

LATIN NAME:
*Eudyptes chrysolophus*
HEIGHT:
76 cm
(30 in)
POPULATION:
9 million pairs
DIET:
Fish, krill, and squid
NESTS:
Shallow nests scraped into mud or gravel

**yellow-eyed penguin**

LATIN NAME:
*Megadyptes antipodes*
HEIGHT:
79 cm
(31 in)
POPULATION:
2,000 pairs
DIET:
Fish and squid
NESTS:
Shallow nests on forest floor, made with grass and twigs

Emperor and king penguins have similar orange and

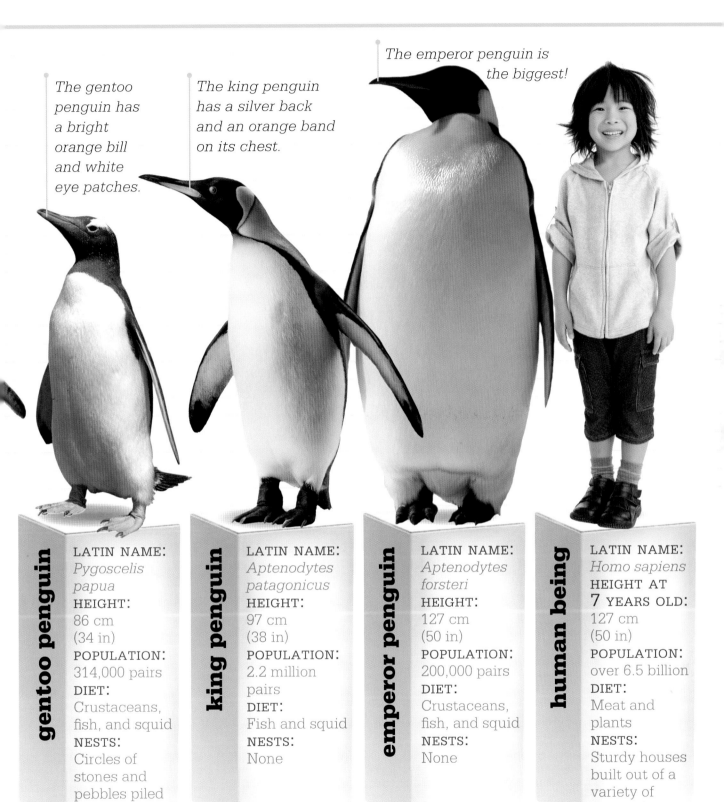

The gentoo penguin has a bright orange bill and white eye patches.

The king penguin has a silver back and an orange band on its chest.

The emperor penguin is the biggest!

**gentoo penguin**

LATIN NAME:
*Pygoscelis papua*
HEIGHT:
86 cm
(34 in)
POPULATION:
314,000 pairs
DIET:
Crustaceans, fish, and squid
NESTS:
Circles of stones and pebbles piled up at the sides

**king penguin**

LATIN NAME:
*Aptenodytes patagonicus*
HEIGHT:
97 cm
(38 in)
POPULATION:
2.2 million pairs
DIET:
Fish and squid
NESTS:
None

**emperor penguin**

LATIN NAME:
*Aptenodytes forsteri*
HEIGHT:
127 cm
(50 in)
POPULATION:
200,000 pairs
DIET:
Crustaceans, fish, and squid
NESTS:
None

**human being**

LATIN NAME:
*Homo sapiens*
HEIGHT AT
**7 YEARS OLD:**
127 cm
(50 in)
POPULATION:
over 6.5 billion
DIET:
Meat and plants
NESTS:
Sturdy houses built out of a variety of materials

yellow colouring, but emperor penguins are much bigger.

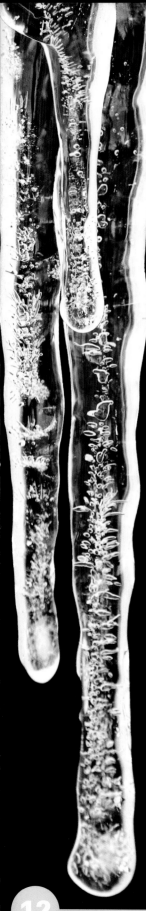

# Penguin homes

Many penguins live in cold seas in the far south of the world. Some land to have chicks on Antarctica and the islands nearby. Other penguins live on the warmer, southern tips of different continents.

*The temperature in Antarctica can fall as low as -70°C (-94°F) – that's very icy.*

*Penguins are found on the coasts of Australia and New Zealand.*

## Cold penguins

Some penguins live around freezing Antarctica and its islands. They spend the slightly warmer summer months on land in order to have their babies.

## Warm penguins

Not all penguins live in cold places. Some live in areas that can get very hot: South America, Africa, Australia, and New Zealand. They spend a lot of time in the water to keep cool.

**Antarctica is the coldest, windiest, driest place on**

*The most northern penguins live on the Galápagos Islands, off South America.*

Australia

**New Zealand**

**PACIFIC OCEAN**

**ROSS SEA**

# Antarctica

**SOUTH POLE**

*A few types of penguins live near, and on, Antarctica itself.*

**INDIAN OCEAN**

**South America**

**WEDDELL SEA**

**ATLANTIC OCEAN**

**Africa**

*Some penguins live at the southern tip of South Africa.*

*Penguins can be found on the coasts of Peru and Chile.*

Earth. Even in the summer months it is very cold.

# Penguins on land

Penguins look very funny when they are on land. They stand completely upright on their two feet, just like we do!

African penguin

## Solid bones

Most birds have hollow, light bones so they can fly. Penguins' bones are solid. This helps them swim but makes them slow on land.

Emperor penguin

## Getting around

### 1 Walking

The bigger the penguin, the slower it walks. Big emperor penguins shuffle slowly across the snow.

### 2 Sliding

Penguins that live on ice find sliding on their tummies easier than walking.

Can you think of any other birds that can't fly?

*Penguins have sharp claws on their webbed feet to help grip ice and rocks.*

**3 Leaping out**

When penguins need to land on steep rocks or icebergs, they swim very fast, then shoot out of the water, almost flying ashore.

**The ostrich is one, but there are many more to discover.**

# Penguins in the sea

Penguins may be slow on land, but they are brilliant swimmers. They are the only flightless birds in the world that can swim underwater.

*Penguins' black, back feathers camouflage them from above when they swim.*

## Flying underwater

Penguins' wings are used as flippers underwater. When they swim they flap them, just as flying birds flap their wings. They use their feet to steer, and they can dart around at great speeds.

*Their white tummy feathers camouflage them from below.*

## Holding their breath

Just like you and me, penguins can't breathe underwater. They have to hold their breath and swim to the surface to breathe. Emperor penguins can hold their breath for 18 minutes!

*Penguins have excellent eyesight, which is very useful in deep, dark water.*

 **Find out more**
about the fastest swimmer on page 54.

**Emperor penguins can dive to depths of 500 metres**

## Penguin paddles

Penguins have webbed feet, which help them paddle on the surface of the water. They row with their flippers, like a person paddling a kayak.

*Penguins look a little like ducks when they swim on the surface.*

## Underwater naps

Some penguins spend up to nine months in the ocean. Nobody knows how they sleep. Scientists think they must take short naps at or beneath the surface.

**(1,640 feet) when swimming to catch fish – that's deep!**

# Leaping and diving

Penguins swim very fast underwater, but if they really want to pick up speed, they "porpoise". They leap out of the water, take a quick breath, fly over the waves, then duck just beneath the surface again. Penguins can travel like this for many miles.

**Penguins look a little like dolphins when they**

porpoise. Sometimes they do it to flee from danger.

# Penguin feathers

Penguin bodies are perfectly adapted to cold, which is why they can survive in places that most animals can't. Their feathers keep them warm and dry.

Moulting king penguin

### Feathers

Penguin feathers look like other birds' feathers, but they are smaller and packed closer together. They overlap like roof tiles to keep the cold air out. Fluffy strands at the bottom of the feathers are for extra warmth.

To cover these two pages in penguin feathers, you

## The moult

Penguin feathers get worn out. So each year penguins moult – their feathers fall out. They have to stay on land until their new feathers grow in. This can sometimes take a month.

**Find out more** about moulting chicks on page 52.

*Old feathers are pushed out by the new ones and are left in a huge pile on the ground.*

*Penguins have about 100 feathers per square inch!*

## Oiling feathers

Penguins have special glands near their tails that produce oil. They use their beaks to spread the oil all over their feathers to make them waterproof.

*Oil is made in penguins' bodies and emerges from this little hole by their tails.*

**would need about 8,000 of them!**

21

# The iceberg café

Welcome to the iceberg café! On the menu today are all the delicious sea creatures that penguins love to eat. Penguins only feed in the water.

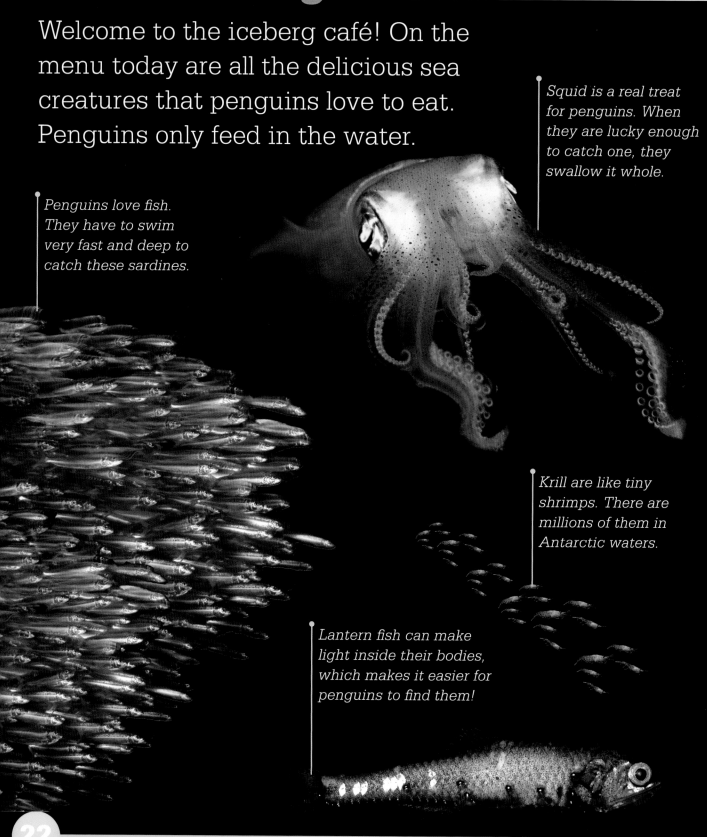

*Squid is a real treat for penguins. When they are lucky enough to catch one, they swallow it whole.*

*Penguins love fish. They have to swim very fast and deep to catch these sardines.*

*Krill are like tiny shrimps. There are millions of them in Antarctic waters.*

*Lantern fish can make light inside their bodies, which makes it easier for penguins to find them!*

**Penguins sometimes have to travel for hundreds of**

Penguins have to hold their breath and dive to catch fish.

**ICEBERG CAFÉ**

## Salty drinks

Penguins drink seawater, which is salty. They have special glands in their bodies that take out the salt.

## Spiky tongues

Penguins don't have teeth. Instead, they have spikes on their beaks and tongues to grip slippery fish.

## CATCH OF THE DAY

| | | |
|---|---|---|
| sardines | anchovies | squid |
| lantern fish | krill | crabs |

## Children's menu

Penguin chicks eat exactly the same food that the adults do. The adult swallows the food, which gets mashed up in its stomach. Then the adult regurgitates, or coughs it up, for the chick.

kilometres to find fish.

# Danger!

On land and at sea, penguins have to look out for danger. There are vicious predators ready to grab them for a meal.

## Orcas

Orcas love to eat penguins, which they prey on in the sea. They have also been known to wobble icebergs back and forth, tipping the penguins sitting on top into the ocean!

*Orcas are sometimes known as killer whales, but they are actually the largest dolphins.*

24

## Gulls and skuas

Birds such as gulls and skuas steal penguin eggs and will take small chicks if they are left alone by their parents. Chicks and eggs are in big danger on land, particularly in warmer climates where mammals live and hunt.

*This kelp gull has snatched a gentoo penguin egg and is carrying it away.*

## People

Unfortunately, the biggest danger to penguins is us, humans. This penguin is covered in oil that has spilled from a boat.

**Find out more** about the effects of an oil spill on page 42.

*Leopard seals can grow to 3.5 metres (11½ feet) in length.*

## Leopard seals

Penguins are leopard seals' favourite and most important meal. The seals lurk in the water near penguins' breeding grounds and grab them when the penguins feed at sea.

# Galápagos penguins

Galápagos penguins live on islands much further north than any other penguins do. They are the rarest penguins in the world.

⚠️ **UNDER THREAT (see page 74)**

*Galápagos penguins swim in the water during the day and sleep on land at night.*

## Galápagos Islands

The Galápagos Islands, off South America, lie on the Equator. The weather on the islands gets hot, but the Pacific Ocean that surrounds them is very cool, which the penguins like.

*Because it is always warm on the islands, these penguins can have their chicks at any time of year.*

**GALÁPAGOS**

*Spheniscus mendiculus*

**HEIGHT**
51 cm (20 in)

**BREEDING AREA**
Galápagos Islands

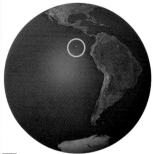

▣ Island populations
▢ Mainland populations

**POPULATION**
1,000 pairs

**FEATURES**
Small body with long bill; white ring around the face.

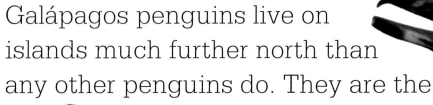

## Watch out – hawk!

Galápagos penguins share their islands with lots of animals, some of which are very dangerous to the penguins and their chicks.

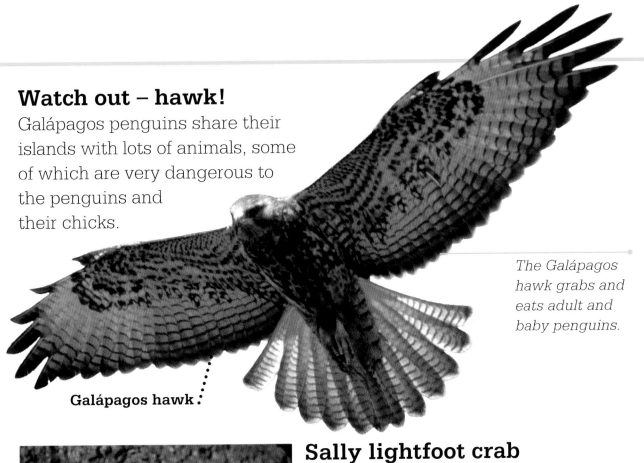

*The Galápagos hawk grabs and eats adult and baby penguins.*

**Galápagos hawk**

## Sally lightfoot crab

This Sally lightfoot crab likes penguin eggs for lunch. It will even take a small chick if a parent leaves it alone for too long.

**Sally lightfoot crab**

# Humboldt penguins

Both of the penguins on these pages are from South America. Penguins that live in warmer areas share their habitat with people and many other types of animals, too.

## Fighting for space

### Fishing rights

Humboldt penguins compete with people for fish. If fishing boats catch too many in their nets, the penguins don't have enough.

### Beach sharing

Humboldt penguins often have to share their nesting grounds with other birds and animals.

*This penguin made a nest below a pelican colony!*

**HUMBOLDT**
*Spheniscus humboldti*

**HEIGHT**
74 cm (29 in)

**BREEDING AREA**
Coastlines of Peru and Chile, South America

Antarctica

○ *Island populations*
　*Mainland populations*

**POPULATION**
6,000 pairs

**FEATURES**
Single black chest band; bare face showing pink skin

**Humboldt and Magellanic penguins look similar.**

# Magellanic penguins

Penguins that live around South America are thinner than Antarctic penguins becuase they don't need as much blubber to keep them warm.

## Mate for life

Like most penguins, when Magellanic penguins meet their mates, they stay together for life.

**MAGELLANIC**

*Spheniscus magellanicus*

**HEIGHT**
74 cm (29 in)

**BREEDING AREA**
Cool coasts of Chile and Argentina

Antarctica

○ Island populations
▢ Mainland populations

**POPULATION**
1.3 million pairs

**FEATURES**
Two black chest bands – one under the chin and one below.

▶▶ **Find out more**
about courting penguins on page 48.

**Compare the bands of black across their chests.**

# The giant penguin

Imagine a penguin almost as big as an adult human! One existed a long time ago.

**Peru**

The giant penguin fossil was found in Peru, South America.

Peru

*The giant penguin stood 1.5 m (5 ft) tall.*

*The average height of a man is about 1.75 m (5 ft, 9 in).*

*The emperor penguin is the biggest penguin living today.*

*An emperor penguin can be bigger than a seven-year-old child.*

**Odd giant**

Today, the larger the penguin, the further south it lives. It is strange to have found the biggest penguin living so far north.

**This extinct penguin has just been discovered.**

## Giant fossil

In 2010, the fossil of a giant penguin was found in the ground. Scientists think that it lived on Earth 36 million years ago, when Peru was lots of islands rather than part of a continent.

*The giant penguin had a much longer beak than penguins today have.*

*Scientists think that the penguin speared fish with its 18-cm-long (7-in-long) beak.*

## Water king

The official name for the giant penguin is *Inkayacu paracasensis*. But it is commonly known as the "water king".

*The fossil showed that the penguin had more grey feathers than white.*

## Deep diver

Among living birds, the heavier the penguin, the deeper it can dive. So the water king could probably dive very deep.

**Perhaps there are even bigger ones yet to be found!**

# Royal penguins

The next eight pages will introduce the six crested penguins, starting with royal penguins. Crested penguins all have yellow head feathers.

## Macquarie Island

Royal penguins live at sea for the chilly winter months. In the summer, they head to just one place, Macquarie Island, between New Zealand and the Antarctic, to breed.

**ROYAL**
*Eudyptes schlegeli*

**HEIGHT**
76 cm (30 in)

**BREEDING AREA**
Macquarie Island – halfway between New Zealand and Antarctica

Antarctica

◉ Island populations
▢ Mainland populations

**POPULATION**
850,000 pairs

**FEATURES**
White face and chin, black back, and yellow head crests

*Royal penguin colonies are so crowded that all the plants are trampled by the end of the breeding season.*

There are six types of crested penguin. See if you can

# Erect-crested penguins

Erect-crested penguins got their name because they are the only penguins whose crests stand up.

⚠️ **UNDER THREAT** (see page 74)

## Mystery penguins

These penguins are spotted on islands where they come to breed between September and May. When they return to sea, they disappear. No one knows exactly where they go in the ocean.

*Very few people have studied these penguins, so not much is known about them.*

| ERECT-CRESTED |
|---|
| *Eudyptes sclateri* |
| **HEIGHT** |
| 71 cm (28 in) |
| **BREEDING AREA** |
| A few islands south of New Zealand |
| Antarctica |
| ◉ *Island populations*<br>　 *Mainland populations* |
| **POPULATION** |
| 83,000 pairs |
| **FEATURES** |
| Black face and yellow crests that can stand up high; chocolate-brown eyes |

learn to tell which is which by their crests.

# Rockhopper penguins

Rockhoppers are small crested penguins that live on rocky islands. They are very good at jumping and climbing on steep cliffs.

*Rockhoppers' eyes are much brighter red than other crested penguins' eyes.*

**Yellow crest**

**ROCKHOPPER**
*Eudyptes chrysocome*

**HEIGHT**
58 cm (23 in)

**BREEDING AREA**
Many islands all around Antarctica and the tip of South America

Antarctica

◎ Island populations
▢ Mainland populations   –

**POPULATION**
1.2 million pairs

**FEATURES**
Black and white body; yellow crests above tiny bright red eyes; spiky, black head feathers.

**Rockhoppers look like the macaroni penguins on page**

## Surfing

Rockhoppers wait for a big wave and then "surf" onto rocks, landing with a bump.

## Climbing

These penguins are excellent at hopping up steep cliffs, which is how they got their name.

## Jumping

Rockhoppers jump off cliffs feet first into the water, rather than head first like other penguins do.

*Rockhoppers are regularly monitored to try to find out why their numbers are decreasing each year.*

## Noisy birds

Rockhopper penguins live in small groups, but they are incredibly noisy. They fight over nesting materials.

⚠ UNDER THREAT (see page 74)

**38. Compare their crests. Can you see the differences?**

# Fiordland penguins

Not much is known about Fiordland penguins because they are timid and avoid people. They breed on the south island of New Zealand.

### Rainforest penguins

Fiordland penguins breed in the cool rainforest, nesting under boulders and in caves. Their biggest danger is the animals that people have brought to the island, such as cats and dogs.

*Fiordland penguins are known as tawaki in the Maori language of New Zealand.*

**FIORDLAND**

*Eudyptes pachyrhynchus*

**HEIGHT**
61 cm (24 in)

**BREEDING AREA**
Rainforests on the southern island of New Zealand

Antarctica

⊙ Island populations
▢ Mainland populations

**POPULATION**
3,000 pairs

**FEATURES**
Yellow crests that start at the bill and sweep back over the eyes; dark blue head

**There are not very many of either of these penguins in**

# Snares penguins

Snares penguins breed on the Snares Islands, just south of New Zealand. There are no mammals on the islands, so the penguins are in little danger there.

## Protected penguins

There aren't many Snares penguins left on the islands, so the New Zealand government has forbidden people to visit them.

*Penguins that live in warmer areas hold their wings out and fluff up their feathers to keep cool.*

**SNARES**
*Eudyptes robustus*

**HEIGHT**
66 cm (26 in)

**BREEDING AREA**
Snares Islands, south of New Zealand

Antarctica

○ *Island populations*
  *Mainland populations*

**POPULATION**
29,000 pairs

**FEATURES**
Thin yellow crests that run from the bill over the top of the eye; white skin beneath the bill

**the world, but their numbers are not going down.**

# Macaroni penguins

There are more macaroni penguins in the world than any other penguin. Scientists estimate there are about 18 million macaronis alive today!

*Macaroni penguins are the largest of the crested penguins.*

## Waving macaronis

Macaronis wave their heads backwards and forwards and screech loudly when they are looking for mates.

**MACARONI**
*Eudyptes chrysolophus*

**HEIGHT**
76 cm (30 in)

**BREEDING AREA**
Tip of South America and the islands surrounding Antarctica

Antarctica

⊙ Island populations
▪ Mainland populations

**POPULATION**
9 million pairs

**FEATURES**
Black face; large orangy-yellow crests that meet right between the eyes

How can you spot a macaroni? Its two big orange crests

▶▶ **Find out more**
about penguin
eggs on page 50.

## Nests
Macaroni nests are often
made in clumps of grass.

## Eggs
Macaronis lay two eggs
together every year, but
they kick the first egg
out of the nest when
the second is laid.
Only one
hatches.

## Macaroni hair
Macaroni penguins were
named after 18th-century
British men who wore
extraordinary hairstyles
and were called macaronis.

**meet in the middle of the penguin's forehead.**

# African penguins

**UNDER THREAT**
(see page 74)

African penguins live on the coast of South Africa and on nearby islands.

*African penguins have pink areas around their eyes.*

## Under threat

There are fewer African penguins alive than ever before. So there are laws in South Africa that protect them and make it illegal to harm them.

**AFRICAN**
*Spheniscus demersus*

**HEIGHT**
69 cm (27 in)

**BREEDING AREA**
Southern tip of South Africa and a few nearby islands

Antarctica

▣ Island populations
▢ Mainland populations

**POPULATION**
26,000 pairs

**FEATURES**
Horseshoe-shaped stripe across the chest; pink areas around the eyes

*In some areas you can swim and splash around with wild African penguins.*

## Tourist attraction

Penguins in South Africa share their beaches with people. They are confident birds and are popular with tourists.

**Find out more** about an oil spill that hurt these penguins on the next page.

## Poop nests

These penguins used to make their nests out of their own poop, called guano! These days, people take guano away to help grow crops. The penguins now make nests by burrowing in sand or using twigs.

# OIL SPILL! PENGUIN RESCUE

## DISASTER STRIKES

### Penguin peril

On 23 June 2000, the oil tanker *Treasure* sank between Dassen and Robben islands off the coast of South Africa – home to thousands of African penguins. 1,300 tons of oil spilled into the sea.

1,300 tons of oil seeped from the stricken tanker

## Locals rally to save oil-covered penguins

Oil is deadly to penguins. It is poisonous if they drink it. If the oil gets on their feathers, penguins may no longer be waterproof, and they can freeze. Over 20,000 penguins were covered in oil, and all would have died if local people hadn't come to the rescue. Penguins were collected from the ocean and nursed back to health.

*MORE THAN* **20,000** *penguins were covered in oil*

## The clean up: four steps to a clean penguin

**1**

The penguins were given medicine to clean the oil out of their tummies.

**2**

The feathers were washed with a special soap until all the oil was removed.

**African penguin covered in oil**

## Saved!

Thanks to locals and penguin experts, many penguins were saved.

## The rescue operation

**Help from the local people**

The disaster struck during breeding season, so thousands of chicks were abandoned by their oil-covered parents. The chicks were collected by locals and cared for until their parents were healthy again.

**18,516** penguins were cleaned.

**3,350** penguin chicks were rescued.

*2,000 penguins died, but many more were rescued*

The penguins were fed and brought to swim in tanks until their feathers became waterproof.

After a couple of weeks, the penguins were released into the wild.

**43**

# Yellow-eyed penguins

Yellow-eyed penguins are the only species with yellow eyes. They are in the greatest danger of becoming extinct because their habitat is threatened. Their numbers are constantly going down.

⚠️ **UNDER THREAT** (see page 74)

## Ancient penguin

Yellow-eyed penguins live in forests in New Zealand and some of the islands nearby. They are thought to be the oldest penguin species. They are now under threat because of people cutting down their forest homes.

---

**YELLOW-EYED**

*Megadyptes antipodes*

**HEIGHT**
79 cm (31 in)

**BREEDING AREA**
South coast of New Zealand and nearby islands

Antarctica

⊙ Island populations
▢ Mainland populations

**POPULATION**
2,000 pairs

**FEATURES**
Yellow eyes and yellow eye stripes across the head; they are not crested penguins

**Turn to page 74 to find out how people are trying to**

# Fairy penguins

Fairy penguins are the smallest penguins. They are also known as little penguins or blue penguins.

*Fairy penguins feed in the water at night and sleep on land by day. Yellow-eyed penguins do the opposite.*

## City penguins

Fairy penguins live in Australia, in New Zealand, and on the surrounding islands. There is even a colony that breeds in Sydney – Australia's biggest city!

*This fairy penguin chick has very blue feathers.*

**FAIRY**
*Eudyptula minor*

**HEIGHT**
46 cm (18 in)

**BREEDING AREA**
South coast of New Zealand, Australia, and small islands

Antarctica

◉ *Island populations*
▢ *Mainland populations*

**POPULATION**
500,000 pairs

**FEATURES**
Blue and grey feathers, and a white stripe around the edge of the flippers

**make sure penguins don't become extinct.**

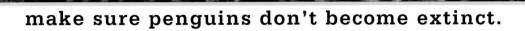

# The colony

When pairs of pengiuns want to breed, they always return to the place they were born. They breed mostly in the summer months, so many of them arrive at the same place at the same time. It can be very crowded and noisy in a penguin colony!

# Nesting

When penguins want to breed, they first find mates. Then each pair finds a safe place to make a nest and keep the eggs.

## Female approval

If the female penguin admires the male's displays, she shows her approval by displaying back to the male.

## Courtship

When a male is looking for a female mate, he performs elaborate displays to females to try to impress them. He flaps his wings, stretches his head, and makes louds calls.

*Chinstrap penguins also hiss when they are courting.*

**Penguin nests are mostly simple and on the ground.**

## Stone nest

Chinstrap penguins make shallow, round nests out of pebbles. Both parents collect the pebbles.

## Grass nest

Yellow-eyed penguins find dips in the ground and line them with grass and twigs.

## Burrows

Magellanic penguins make deep burrows under bushes or find holes in rocks near the coastline.

*The female emperor penguin copies the male.*

## Bowing emperors

Emperor penguins' displays are very impressive. Both penguins stretch up high, make shrill calls, and then bow to each other.

**Find out more** about emperor penguin eggs on page 66.

# Penguin eggs

Female penguins lay the eggs, then both parents sit on them for 30 to 60 days, depending on their species. The eggs then hatch into fluffy chicks.

## Two eggs, one chick

Most penguins lay two eggs, but in almost every species, only one will hatch.

## Tough eggs

Penguin eggs are thicker than other birds' eggs. They are often laid in simple nests – sometimes made of hard rocks – so they need to be thick to keep from breaking.

*An egg will freeze in about five minutes if it is left in the snow. It must be kept warm.*

*Life-sized emperor penguin egg*

*Life-sized African penguin egg*

*Life-sized fairy penguin egg*

**Penguin eggs have large yolks. While a chick is**

### 1 Hatching

The parents take turns sitting on the eggs until one hatches.

### 2 Bonding

The parents bond with the newborn chick so they recognize each other.

### 3 First meal

Penguins have a throat pocket where food is stored for a chick's first meals.

## Egg protection

Penguins eat food only from the sea. The parents take turns going to the water to feed, so an adult is always guarding the egg.

*If the eggs are left alone, they may be eaten by a hungry predator.*

**growing in an egg, it eats the yolk to help it grow.**

# Growing chicks

Penguin parents spend many months working hard to care for their chicks. When the chicks grow waterproof feathers, they can enter the water and feed themselves.

*Nobody knows how a returning parent finds its chick in the noisy crowd!*

### Feeding chicks

Chicks have fluffy baby feathers so they stay on land. Parents take turns bringing their chicks food from the ocean.

### 1 Baby feathers
A chick is born with fluffy feathers that are warm but not waterproof.

### 2 Moulting
In four to nine months, the chick moults. The fluffy feathers fall out.

### 3 Waterproof
New, waterproof feathers grow in. The penguin can now swim.

**When the chick has its adult, waterproof feathers, the**

## Emperor crèches

When the chicks are older, the parents leave to find food together. The chicks are left in huge groups, called crèches, and often huddle together to keep warm.

*Some penguin chicks, such as this emperor chick, look very different from their parents.*

## Fluffy chicks

Most penguin chicks can enter the sea at about four months. But the bigger emperor chicks stay on land for up to a year.

**parents' job is done.**

# Gentoo penguins

⚠️ **UNDER THREAT**
(see page 74)

Gentoo penguins have bright orange bills and feet. They swim near the Antarctic islands and go ashore to nest.

## Fastest penguin

Gentoo penguins are big, and they are the fastest penguins underwater. They can swim at speeds of 36 kilometres per hour (22 miles per hour) – that's faster than a human can run.

### GENTOO

*Pygoscelis papua*

**HEIGHT**
86 cm (34 in)

**BREEDING AREA**
Many islands around Antarctica and a small part of an Antarctic peninsula

Antarctica

⬜ *Island populations*
⬜ *Mainland populations*

**POPULATION**
314,000 pairs

**FEATURES**
Large orange bill, and white patches around the eyes; long, stiff tail feathers that stick out

*It is easy to recognize a gentoo because of the white stripe over the top of its head.*

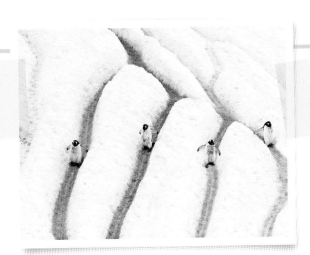

## Penguin highway

Gentoo parents create "roads" in the snow as they travel to the sea and back to get food for their chicks.

## Pebbles

Gentoos make their nests out of pebbles. It is the males' job to collect the pebbles, and they offer them to the females to try to impress them.

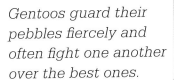

*Gentoos guard their pebbles fiercely and often fight one another over the best ones.*

## Penguin poop

Gentoos have to make sure their poop stays out of the nest, so they shoot the poop away!

## Chicks

Gentoos lay two eggs. Unusually for penguins, both hatch into chicks.

# Chinstrap penguins

A chinstrap penguin is easy to recognize because it has a black stripe beneath its chin that looks like a chinstrap.

*The chinstrap and black head make the penguin look as if it is wearing a helmet!*

## Southern birds

Chinstrap penguins spend their lives swimming in the freezing waters of Antarctica. In the summer, they come ashore to breed on the mainland and the islands nearby.

**CHINSTRAP**

*Pygoscelis antarcticus*

**HEIGHT**
71 cm (28 in)

**BREEDING AREA**
Antarctica and many of the surrounding islands

Antarctica

◉ Island populations
Mainland populations

**POPULATION**
6 million pairs

**FEATURES**
White face with a black line beneath the chin, and a black head; black bill

*Chinstraps climb onto icebergs to keep safe from sea predators such as orcas and leopard seals.*

## Fighting chinstraps

These penguins are bold and can be very aggressive with one another over nesting sites.

## Ice rides

Chinstrap penguins like to ride on icebergs. Sometimes too many climb on, forcing some to fall off into the water.

## Ice climbs

These penguins can climb straight up steep icebergs from the water. They use their feet and flippers to grip on to the ice.

*Chinstraps can even jump big distances to reach a secure foothold.*

**Find out more**

about rockhoppers, which are also good at climbing, on page 34.

# Adélie penguins

Adélie penguins live in the chilly waters around Antarctica. They are strong swimmers, and they sometimes travel more than 100 kilometres (60 miles) to find food.

**ADÉLIE**
*Pygoscelis adeliae*

**HEIGHT**
76 cm (30 in)

**BREEDING AREA**
Around the coast of Antarctic and on a few other very southern islands

Antarctica

**POPULATION**
2.5 million pairs

**FEATURES**
Black head with white eye ring; reddish bill with a black tip; white tummy

## Adélie year

Between March and September, Adélies remain at sea. They rest on icebergs when they are tired. They come ashore in September to breed, stumbling and swimming over tons of sea ice to reach the mainland.

Adélies nest in colonies of up to 200,000 birds. What a loud

*People often think Adélies look as if they are wearing white shirts and tuxedos!*

**Find out more** about how penguins keep warm in the snow on page 20.

## Nesting

Adélies make shallow dips in the ground and surround them with stones. Sometimes it snows so hard that the penguins get buried in the snow, but they still stay sitting on their eggs.

*If a parent leaves its egg, it will freeze and the chick will die.*

## Beach dash

Leopard seals are the Adélies' biggest predator. Seals are not as fast on land as in water, so it is safe for the Adélie to tiptoe past this sleeping seal!

**place that must be!**

# Riding the ice

Freezing Antarctica is a hazardous place for these Adélie penguins. There is danger lurking beneath the chilly water, so the penguins have to find a safe spot.

## Safety on the iceberg

When Adélies breed on the mainland, they must hunt for fish near the shore. Leopard seals are always ready to grab them for a tasty meal, so the penguins find safety on floating sea ice between dives.

# King penguins

King penguins are easy to recognize because of the bright yellow and orange plumage on their heads and necks.

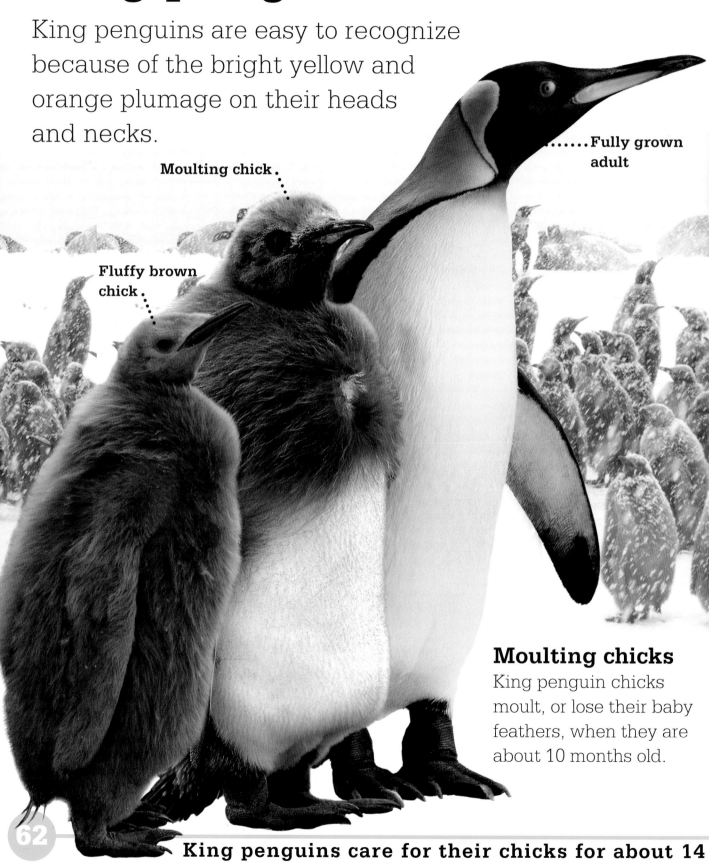

Moulting chick

Fluffy brown chick

.......Fully grown adult

## Moulting chicks
King penguin chicks moult, or lose their baby feathers, when they are about 10 months old.

**King penguins care for their chicks for about 14**

## Beach sharing

King penguins often share their beaches with enormous elephant seals. Luckily the seals don't eat them on land, so they are safe.

*Elephant seals swim fast enough to catch penguins in the water, but they are slow on land.*

**Elephant seal**

**KING**

*Aptenodytes patagonicus*

**HEIGHT**
97 cm (38 in)

**BREEDING AREA**
Islands around Antarctica

**Antarctica**

◉ Island populations
▧ Mainland populations

**POPULATION**
2.2 million pairs

**FEATURES**
Yellow and orange head feathers

## Left in charge

King penguin chicks stay on their parents' feet for up to eight weeks. They then join a crèche. One adult keeps an eye on all the chicks in the crèche!

**Find out more**
about chicks on page 52.

**months – longer than any other bird in the world!**

# The emperors' journey

For thousands of years, emperor penguins have taken an extraordinary journey each year to breed in one of the harshest climates on Earth.

**EMPEROR**
*Aptenodytes forsteri*

**HEIGHT**
127 cm (50 in)

**BREEDING AREA**
All around the edge of mainland Antarctica

Antarctica

- ◉ *Island populations*
- ▢ *Mainland populations*

**POPULATION**
200,000 pairs

**FEATURES**
Large bodies with yellow and orange head feathers

*The penguins must travel over miles and miles of bumpy ice.*

**Follow the incredible journey of the emporer penguin**

### The long walk

At the beginning of the Antarctic winter, emperor penguins walk more than 110 kilometres (70 miles), day and night, without stopping. They head to their breeding ground. Their journey takes about a week.

over the next four pages.

# From emperor egg to chick

## 1 Courtship
After a week of walking, the penguins reach their breeding ground. They choose their mate by calling and bowing to each other.

## 2 The egg
The egg is laid. The mother must now return to the sea to feed, so she passes the egg carefully to the male, who balances it on his feet.

## 5 The immature penguin
In spring, the chick hatches and sits on the father's feet to keep warm. When the mother returns, she moves the chick to her feet and feeds it.

## 6 The father leaves
The male has not eaten for 125 days. The father and chick sing so they can find each other again. He returns to the water.

**Penguin chicks are not taught by their parents to swim**

### 3 Father huddle

As the temperature drops and winds howl around them, the fathers huddle together to keep warm through the winter. They sleep standing up.

### 4 The mother feeds

Meanwhile, the mothers have reached the water. They feed themselves so they can look after their chicks. They must watch for danger as they swim.

### 7 Feeding the chick

The parents take turns going to the water for food for about two months. When the baby is big enough, the adults travel together, leaving the baby.

### 8 Chick huddle

While the parents are walking back to the water to find food, the fluffy chicks huddle together in groups to keep warm.

**or hunt in water. They instinctively know how to do it.**

# All grown up

As the weather gets slightly warmer in Antarctica, the ice melts and the emperor penguin breeding ground is nearer to the ocean. The chicks have only a short journey to the edge of the ice for their first plunge.

## The final plunge

After nine months working together, the parents have completed their job. The chicks remain on land for another two months while they moult. When their adult feathers have grown in, they travel to the sea and can now feed themselves.

# Interview

**Name:** Cherry Alexander
**Nationality:** British
**Profession:** Polar photographer

**Q When did you start taking photographs?**

**A** I used one of my father's old cameras from the age of eight. I had my own serious camera when I was 12.

**Q How do you travel to Antarctica?**

**A** I fly to the south of South America or Australia and take a strong boat down to the ice.

**Q What made you want to photograph penguins in Antarctica?**

**A** My first trip to Antarctica was to an emperor penguin colony and I thought they were magical. I was hooked.

*Taking pictures*
*Luckily, penguins go on land to have chicks in the summer, when it is light all day for taking photos.*

# with a photographer

**Q  Do you camp in the snow?**

A  No, I sleep on the boat in a cosy cabin!

**Q  Do you wear special warm clothes?**

A  In the Antarctic summer, I wear normal winter clothes. But if it is very cold, I wear thermal underwear and a down jacket with big boots.

**Q  Are the penguins scared of you?**

A  Not really; the adults are very busy building nests and feeding babies. If I move slowly, they ignore me. The babies are often very curious and walk up to have a good look at me.

**Q  Are penguins noisy?**

A  One pair of penguins doesn't make much noise, but several hundred together can be very noisy!

**Q  Have you been pecked by a penguin?**

A  No, but one tried to eat my boot once – it didn't hurt.

**Q  Is a penguin colony smelly?**

A  A colony looks very clean and doesn't smell before the snow melts. But once the chicks are half grown and standing in their poop, it can smell pretty bad. But they aren't nearly as smelly as elephant seals!

**Q  Which is your favourite penguin?**

A  Normally the last one I spent time with! The emperors are so big and calm. The Adélies are so small and fearless. The gentoos are quiet and gentle – until they get into a fight. I love them all!

Emperor penguin

# A winning photo

In 1995, Cherry Alexander won an award for this amazing photo of chinstrap penguins on an iceberg.

## The perfect picture

Taking photographs is not only about having a good camera. Photographers learn how to use the light around them, and they must be very patient. It can take weeks of waiting to get a fantastic photograph of penguins, like this one.

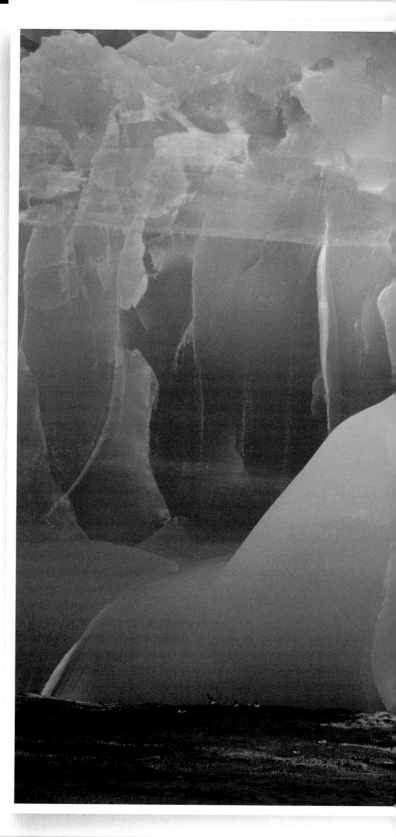

*Freezing and defrosting can damage a camera. Photographers have to take care in extreme cold.*

**Animals are difficult to photograph because they move**

a lot! Try taking pictures of your garden wildlife.

# Protecting penguins

People have put penguins in danger by building on their breeding grounds and introducing animals that kill them. Today people around the world are working hard to build penguins a better future.

The Galápagos penguin is still under threat, but it may soon be off the endangered list.

The Galápagos Islands have many new laws to protect their penguins.

## Protected sites

Some countries have made special laws that protect penguins. They make sure people don't take too many fish from where penguins live, and they keep people from visiting when the chicks are young.

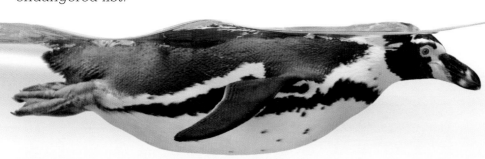

## Zoos

Zoos often breed penguins. The keepers study them as they grow, which helps them to understand how penguins behave. This is very useful knowledge when protecting them in the wild.

**Most penguin species are "at risk". But six are endangered,**

**UNDER THREAT**

# Endangered

These six penguins are endangered. Look through the book for the yellow signs to see which ones they are.

## Saving fairies

To make sure fairy penguins don't become endangered, local people in Sydney Harbour, Australia, are working to protect the 60 pairs that breed there.

*The fairy penguin breeding site is watched and kept free of predators.*

*The penguins are tagged so they can be studied throughout the year.*

*Humboldt penguins are one of the most common species found and bred in zoos.*

**Find out more** about how an oil spill harmed penguins on page 42.

**75**

**which means in danger of becoming extinct.**

# Glossary

**Antarctica**
The continent centred around the South Pole. Most of Antarctica is covered in ice.

**blubber**
The layer of fat under the skin of an animal that helps keep it warm.

**burrow**
A hole in the ground made or used by an animal as a home.

**camouflage**
Natural colouring that allows animals to hide by making them look like their surroundings.

**chick**
A very young bird.

**colony**
A large group of animals that live together.

**crèche**
A group of young animals gathered in one place for care and protection by one or more adults.

**crest**
A tuft of feathers on the top of a bird's head.

**crustacean**
A sea creature that has an outer skeleton, such as a crab.

**endangered**
At risk of dying out.

**Equator**
An imaginary line that runs around the centre of the Earth and is an equal distance from the North and South Poles.

**extinct**
No longer found alive; known only about through fossils or history.

**flock**
A group of birds of one kind that live, travel, and feed together.

**fossil**
A bone, shell, or other trace of animal or plant from millions of years ago, preserved as rock.

**guano**
The dung of seabirds, used as a fertilizer.

*King penguins in the Falkland Islands head to the water.*

### iceberg
A large mass of ice that has broken off from a glacier and is floating in the sea.

### krill
Tiny, shrimp-like sea creatures.

### mammal
A warm-blooded animal that has hair or fur. Female mammals make milk to feed their young.

### moult
To lose old feathers so that new ones can grow.

### nest
A safe place built by birds, where they lay eggs and take care of their young.

### oil
A thick, greasy liquid that does not mix with water.

### orca
A large ocean mammal. Also called a killer whale.

### plumage
The feathers of a bird.

### polar
Near or having to do with the icy regions around the North or South Pole.

### population
The total number of a species living.

### porpoise
An ocean mammal like a dolphin, with a rounded head and a short, blunt snout. It gives its name to the way that penguins swim quickly through the water.

### rainforest
A dense, tropical forest where a lot of rain falls for much of the year.

### waterproof
Not letting water through.

### webbed feet
Toes that are connected by a web or fold of skin.

### yolk
The yellow part of an egg.

# Index

*Emperor penguin
chicks huddle
for warmth.*

# Thank you